Punk Monkey Productions Presents:

PL.A.Y Noir - 2013

PL.A.Y Noir - 2013

edited by
JAMES ELDEN

A Punk Monkey Productions Publication

PL.A.Y NOIR — 2013

No part of this publication may be reproduced or transmitted in any form or by any means, electronic or mechanical, including photocopy, recording, or any information storage or retrieval systems now known to be invented, without permission in writing from the publishers.

NOTE: All plays contained in this volume are fully protected under the Copyright Laws of the United States of America, the British Empire, including the Dominion of Canada, and all other countries of the International Copyright Union and the Universal Copyright Convention. Permission to reproduce, wholly or in part, by any method, must be obtained from the copyright owners or their agents.

SPECIAL NOTE: Each play contained within this volume is available for individual production and performance with the permission granted by the respected playwright, agent or manager. In addition, the plays contained within this, and subsequent volumes, are available for production and performance, in part, whole or combination of their respected volume and other volumes, under the umbrella of Punk Monkey Productions and PL.A.Y Noir. (See NOTE FROM EDITOR segment for more information.)

Copyright ©2016 by Punk Monkey Productions
All Rights Reserved
ISBN-13: 978-0692806524
ISBN-10: 0692806520

Cover art by Richard Lee Warren

Punk Monkey Productions
North Hollywood, CA

First Punk Monkey Productions Printing, 2016

To Annie and Bernie

CONTENTS

Introduction ix

Note from the Editor xiii

Speak No Evil 1
  by Michael W. Moon

Desperate Desires 25
  by David Galanter

Stiff 37
  by Hope Thompson

The Zone Ranger 61
  by Ben Goldstein
    and Mac Taylor

INTRODUCTION

I find one of the most appealing aspects of producing Noir for the stage is its ability to lend itself to simplicity. That's not to say Noir itself is simple; on the contrary, Noir in its original (read truest) form is quite complex and sometimes downright confusing.

Delving into the roots of Noir, back to the vintage crime novels of Raymond Chandler, Dashiell Hammett, and James M. Cain, just keeping character's names straight, not to mention their link to the case at hand, presents the reader with a bit of a challenge, especially in a day and age of dwindling attention spans. Chandler's *The Big Sleep* was a combination of two shorter stories, so remembering which plotline a character pertained to and whether or not they were connected to a new subplot sometimes requires returning to pages read to re-familiarize oneself with the story at hand (quite a chore indeed for readers who enjoy the pastime intermittently).

Noir films provided similar obstacles, as well, but offered convenient summarizations in wellplaced monologues within the movie. In *The Maltese Falcon*, Sam Spade's (Humphrey Bogart) retelling of the ship incident that led to the delivery of the coveted package by the vessel's captain is just short of requiring a degree in criminology in order to connect the dots to keep up with the plot.

So in these regards, there is nothing simple about Noir. The simplicity I speak of lies in its staging. Noir as a genre in the theatre, especially black-box and limited-budget productions, requires very little to establish location and period. A detective's office requires little more than a small desk and two chairs (throw in a liquor cabinet for taste); a seedy bar achieved with little more than a few stools and simple counter. A lone, lamp post up-center works wonders for a shady, city street corner. Throw in a dash of 1930s or 40s jazz and vintage wardrobe, and you're well on your way to a great Noir play. Separate all of the above into quadrants on the stage, and scene changes are all but eliminated.

Plays set in a single location are of even greater ease. Hope Thompson's *Stiff*, included in this volume, required little more than a couch and arm chair for its isolated setting. We added an area rug and coat rack for effect, placed the window as the fourth wall, and voila, the den in "mad professor" Crenshaw's mansion.

A great point of study is Michael W. Moon's play *Speak No Evil* (also in this volume). I recommend you try staging it in the simplest way in your head while you read it, then view the film version through the link included with this book.

The latter requires much more aesthetically, especially in Dash's office for example.

Noir on stage allows the audience to fill in the details with their imagination making it somewhat participatory. I suppose this was one of the reasons we set out to make PL.A.Y Noir an ongoing endeavor, not only to bring more of an appreciation to the genre, but to bring the audience and performers that much closer together. I hope that you are able to share the same experience with your audiences.

- **James Elden**

Note from the editor

Each year of PL.A.Y Noir is, in and of itself, a collection of individual one-act plays originally produced in the span of one evening and performed over the course of four weeks. With the publication of this anthology, it is our intention to share these plays with other actors, directors and producers, allowing them to stage their own evening of Noir. As more *PL.A.Y Noir* publications become available, it will allow not only the production of a particular volume, it also uniquely frees the producer to mix and match plays from other *PL.A.Y Noir* collections in order to achieve a particular theme or taste; whether that be comedic, classic, neo, dramatic or any combinations thereof.

For amateur and professional productions that do wish to stage multiple titles within these collections and under the *PL.A.Y Noir* name, know that it too is subject to a royalty and is fully protected under the copyright laws of the United States of America, and of all countries covered by the International Copyright Union (including the Dominion of Canada and the rest of the British Commonwealth), and of all countries covered by the Pan-American Copyright Convention and the Universal Copyright Convention, the Berne Convention, and of all countries with which the United States has reciprocal copyright relations. All rights, including professional and amateur stage performing rights, motion picture, recitation, lecturing, public reading, radio broadcasting, television, video or sound recording, all other forms of mechanical or electronic reproduction, such as CD-ROM, DVD-ROM, information storage or retrieval systems, and photocopying, and the rights of translation into foreign languages, are strictly reserved.

All inquiries concerning rights to multiple titles and the use of the *PL.A.Y Noir* name should be addressed to James Elden via email at info@punkmonkeyproductions.com.

Additional note: Due to the ability to bring the entire cast together as an ensemble, it was our original intention to end each year's production with *The Zone Ranger*. In order to include more of a variety, the idea was abandoned after our 2013 season. Since *The Zone Ranger* was part of our 2013 season, we decided to include it in 2013's publication to keep the integrity of the lineup despite its original printing in *PL.A.Y Noir 2012*. We hope you enjoy revisiting it.

Speak No Evil
By Michael W. Moon

Speak No Evil by Michael W. Moon. Copyright © 2013 by Michael W. Moon. All rights reserved. Reprinted by permission of the author.

CAUTION/ADVICE Professionals and amateurs are hereby warned that performance of this play is subject to a royalty. It is fully protected under the copyright laws of the United States of America, and of all countries covered by the International Copyright Union (including the Dominion of Canada and the rest of the British Commonwealth), and of all countries covered by the Pan-American Copyright Convention and the Universal Copyright Convention, the Berne Convention, and of all countries with which the United States has reciprocal copyright relations. All rights, including professional and amateur stage performing rights, motion picture, recitation, lecturing, public reading, radio broadcasting, television, video or sound recording, all other forms of mechanical or electronic reproduction, such as CD-ROM, DVD-ROM, information storage or retrieval systems, and photocopying, and the rights of translation into foreign languages, are strictly reserved.

All inquiries concerning rights should be addressed to Punk Monkey Productions via email at info@punkmonkeyproductions.

Michael W. Moon

Michael W. Moon is a playwright and designer working in Chicago. After 30 years in theatre he began writing for the stage. He has had readings and staged performances of his pieces performed in Chicago, Boston, Dallas, North Carolina, L.A. and New York. He continues to write and design for the stage.

Speak No Evil was originally produced by Punk Monkey Productions at the Actors Workout Studio in the North Hollywood Arts District in April 2013. It was directed by Christopher Flowers. The lighting design was by Shaunessy Quinn. The cast was as follows:

Harold Newcomb	Andrew J. Hillis
Dash Morgan	Adam Hunter Howard
Frank Banning	Art Oden
Kitten Malone	Sarah Kelly
Joey Numbers	Michael C. Silva
Bartender	Jim Shipley
Detective Matthews	James Elden

CHARACTERS:

HAROLD NEWCOMB
DASH MORGAN
FRANK BANNING
KITTEN MALONE
JOEY NUMBERS
BARTENDER
DETECTIVE MATTHEWS

Night. There is a raggedy man, Harold Newcomb, on one side of the stage selling pencils and sundries from a tray around his neck. A sign on the front of the tray says "PLEASE HELP: I AM MUTE." He stands, barley awake.

Frank comes in from the other side of the stage pulling Joey by the arm.

Kitten is following Joey.

Harold sees them enter and ducks back out of sight when Frank begins yelling.

FRANK: Are you going to tell me what I want to know?

Frank slaps Joey.

KITTEN: Stop it, Frank! Stop it!

JOEY: I told you over and over. I don't know nothing.

Frank pulls a gun from his coat.

JOEY: I swear, Frank! I swear!

Frank begins to pistol whip Joey.

KITTEN: Frank! You're going to kill him!

Joey collapses on the floor.

Frank kicks him in the side.

Frank takes a handkerchief from his coat pocket and wipes his hands and face. He puts the gun back in his jacket.

FRANK: I told you not to cross me. You only got what you deserved. *(He throws the handkerchief at Joey.)* Clean yourself up.

Joey doesn't move.

KITTEN: Frankie. You killed him. I knew it. I knew you were hitting him too hard.

FRANK: Shut up, Kitten. Shut up, or you'll get some of the same.

KITTEN: But Frank?

FRANK: Shut up, I said! *(He goes to Joey and nudges him with his foot.)* Get up, you louse! Get up before I get mad and really let you have it. *(He bends down and grabs Joey's lapels and shakes him.)* Wake up, you bum. I didn't hit you that hard!

Frank shakes him again and then drops him to the ground.

Joey is listless and does not move.

KITTEN: You killed him! Oh, God, Frank, you killed him!

FRANK: Shut up!

Frank reaches down and opens Joey's coat pulling out a large bundle of cash wrapped in brown paper.

Frank leafs through the bundle and then reaches again for Joey's wallet and puts that, along with the cash, in his own coat.

Frank pushes Joey over onto his stomach and stands.

FRANK: I got to get out of town, at least until the heat blows over. You'd better scram, too.

KITTEN: Take me with you, Frankie.

FRANK: I ain't taking no dame with me while I'm on the lam. *(He goes to her and grabs her by the shoulders.)* Forget what you saw here. Don't tell nobody. If you do…

Frank squeezes her arm.

Kitten tries to pull away.

KITTEN: Oww, Frankie, that hurts.

FRANK: It'll hurt a lot more if you open your mouth.

KITTEN: But Frankie?

Frank pushes her away.

FRANK: Beat it. I got to stash the body.

Blackout.

Lights up on a desk with Detective Dash Morgan sitting with his feet on the desk.

He is flipping a coin in the air.

The coin lands in his hand, and he covers it.

DASH: Heads. *(He uncovers the coin.)* Ain't that my luck. No dinner tonight.

There is a knock at the door.

DASH: Come in.

No one enters.

There is another knock on the door.

DASH: Come in, I said.

Again, no one enters.

Another knock.

DASH: Oh, for Pete's sake.

Dash gets up from the desk and goes offstage.

DASH: *(Offstage.)* Can I help you? *(Silence.)* Listen, buddy, I already give to the Salvation Army. *(Silence.)* Yeah, I'm a detective. *(Silence.)* Stop writing on that notepad, and come inside.

Dash leads Harold into the room.

DASH: What can I do for you? What's your name, fella?

Harold writes on his notepad and hands him the paper. Dash takes the paper.

DASH: Mr. Harold Newcomb. I am a mute. I cannot talk.

Dash stops reading.

DASH: All right, Mr. Newcomb. Why don't you have a seat and tell me what it is I can do for you.

Harold sits and writes on his pad.

Dash is already over this method of communicating.

Harold hands him the paper.

Dash reads.

DASH: You want me to investigate a murder.

He looks at Harold.

DASH: Whose murder would we be talking...I mean writing about?

Harold writes on his pad.

DASH: This is going to take forever.

Harold hands him the paper.

DASH: You don't know his name.

Dash crumples the piece of paper and throws it.

DASH: Listen, is this some kind of a joke? Did Matthews in homicide put you up to this? That no good son of a... You an actor or something? I have to say, the costume and the silent treatment are pretty convincing.

Harold writes on his pad then hands it to Dash.

Harold pulls a rolled up notebook from his coat and offers it to Dash.

DASH: This is no joke. Please read this.

Dash takes the notebook, opens it and reads out loud.

DASH: On Tuesday, March 15th I was standing at the corner of Alameda and East Dominguez Street. I stand there most evenings to catch the people coming out of the bars up and down Alameda so I can sell my goods. At about 10:30, two men and a woman come out of the Tick-Tock Lounge. One of the men was named Frankie, he was roughing up another man who I never caught his name. The woman was watching and was getting very upset. This man, Frankie, slapped the guy, and then started pistol-whipping him. Eventually, the man collapsed, and he never got up. Frankie took something out of the man's coat. It was a bundle wrapped in brown paper. When he opened it, it was full of money. He yelled at the woman to leave, and then dragged the body down the alley and ran down Alameda towards downtown. When he had left, I went down the alley, and the body was leaning against a trash can, dead. I got the bartender at the place around the corner to call the police.

Dash stops reading.

DASH: Did you stick around and tell the cops what you saw?

Harold writes on his pad.

DASH: *(Reading.)* I did, but they didn't believe me. They said I did it, and I'm a suspect.

Dash gets up from sitting on the corner of his desk.

DASH: So you want me to act as the go-between and let the cops know what you saw?

Harold writes.

DASH: *(Reading.)* That's right. *(Beat.)* What's in it for me?

Harold writes.

DASH: *(Reading.)* I can't pay you. I am a poor man. *(Beat.)* Listen, Newcomb was it?

Harold shakes his head.

DASH: I'm all for helping out the widows and orphans. I even toss the odd dime into the kettle at Christmas, but I'm not a social worker. I've got overhead, I got an ex-wife and bookie I'm supporting.

Harold writes.

DASH: *(Reading.)* Maybe there's a reward. *(Beat.)* For a two-bit hustler that gets rolled and knocked off by some tough guy? I doubt anybody even picks up the body at the morgue. It's a cruel world out there, Mr. Newcomb, and everybody's in it for themselves, whether you like it or not.

Harold writes.

DASH: *(Reading.)* Isn't there something you can do? *(Beat.)* I don't do charity cases.

Harold clasps his hands together in a silent plea.

DASH: All right. I'll tell you what I'll do. I'll hold on to your little manifesto here and look it over in my spare time. If I come up with anything the cops can bite at, I'll give a call over to a detective friend I have at the precinct. How's that?

Harold starts to write.

DASH: Enough with the writing. Just shake your head yes or no.

Harold nods his head enthusiastically as he grabs Dash's hand and begins pumping it.

DASH: Go home, and don't worry. I'll be in touch if I find anything.

Harold gathers his things and exits.

Dash sits at the desk and opens the notebook.

DASH: Why couldn't it have been some rich, beautiful heiress needing a bodyguard knocking at my door?

Lights fade on Dash.

Lights up on the opposite side of the stage.

A bar counter with stools.

There is a bartender behind the bar.

Kitten is sitting on one of the stools.

She is finishing a drink as the lights rise.

BARTENDER: Do you want another?

KITTEN: Yeah, and don't be stingy with the gin.

Kitten is upset and worried. She is fidgety.

Dash enters and sits next to Kitten who doesn't notice him.

DASH: Excuse me, Miss?

Kitten doesn't look at him.

KITTEN: Get lost.

DASH: And lose the pleasure of your company, Kitten?

KITTEN: What are you doing here, Morgan?

DASH: Looking for you. I've searched all your haunts just hoping I'd find you.

The bartender puts down Kitten's drink.

BARTENDER: You want something?

DASH: Whiskey on the rocks. Put her drink on my tab.

The bartender gives Dash his drink and leaves.

KITTEN: Thanks for the drink. Now beat it.

DASH: Kitten? Is that any way to talk to an old friend?

KITTEN: You're no friend of mine, Morgan. Not after you put my brother away for twenty years in San Quentin.

DASH: I didn't pull the trigger on that bank teller, he did.

KITTEN: What do you want, Morgan?

DASH: A little birdie told me you were part of something ugly the other night, Kitten. Something that could send you to the cell right down the hall from your brother.

KITTEN: I'm not part of anything. Now blow, before I call the cops and report you for harassment.

DASH: I don't think you want the cops knowing what I know. You see, there was a witness the other night outside the Tick-Tock Lounge when your boyfriend, Frankie, got messy and left a stiff leaning against a trashcan.

Kitten takes a long drink and looks through her purse for a cigarette.

DASH: What's a matter, Kitten? You look nervous.

KITTEN: Go peddle your papers somewhere else, Morgan.

She lights a cigarette.

DASH: All right. I will. Maybe down at the precinct. I'm sure Detective Matthews would love to have you in for a chat.

Kitten turns quickly to look at Dash.

KITTEN: Listen, I can't get caught up in this. I got two strikes against me already; another and I land upstate for good. I was just there that's all.

DASH: Sure you were, Kitten. Sure you were.

KITTEN: It got out of hand. I told him to stop.

DASH: Frankie doesn't know how to stop. Where is he, Kitten?

KITTEN: Oh, no you don't. I'm not getting suckered into this by you. You got questions, take them to the library. You're not getting anything out of me.

DASH: I can't help you get clear of this, kid, if you don't help me.

KITTEN: I'm done talking to you. All you ever are to me is trouble.

Kitten gathers her things and leaves.

Dash takes a drink from the glass and empties it.

DASH: Hey, barkeep. Give me another and make it a double.

Lights go down on the bar.

Lights come up opposite.

Kitten is walking down the street.

Frank comes from out of the shadows.

FRANK: Hello, Kitten.

Kitten sees him and runs to him.

KITTEN: Oh, Frankie. I thought you had left town. I was so scared, Frankie. I was so scared.

FRANK: I thought I told you to lay low for a while, Kitten. I thought I told you to get lost.

KITTEN: I couldn't, Frankie. My mother is sick, and there's nobody to take care of her. I've been locked in that house with her. I had to get out.

FRANK: Who you been talking to?

KITTEN: I ain't been talking to nobody.

FRANK: I saw you, Kitten. I saw you talking to that private dick, Morgan.

Frank pulls a gun and points it at Kitten.

FRANK: What did you tell him? What did you say?

KITTEN: I didn't say nothing, Frank. I swear. I didn't say nothing.

FRANK: I wish I could believe you, Kitten.

KITTEN: Frank, I'd never turn you in. I love you, Frank.

FRANK: The cops got a witness, but I can't find out who it is. Is it you? Are you turning on me, Kitten?

KITTEN: Frank, I'd never do that. You know I'd never do that. Let's run, Frank. Let's get out of this town. We'll go up north to Frisco. I got a sister in Frisco. We can hide there.

Kitten moves close and begins to hug and caress Frank.

FRANK: I wish I could believe you. I really do.

KITTEN: But Frank...

Frank shoots Kitten.

Kitten falls to the ground.

FRANK: I can't leave any loose ends, kid.

Frank runs off.

Dash comes running onstage after Frank clears.

He bends down and picks Kitten up from the ground.

DASH: Kitten! Kitten! Who was it? Who shot you?

KITTEN: It was Frankie. I thought he loved me...I thought...

She dies.

DASH: Sleep easy, kid. He won't get away with this.

Lights out on Dash.

Harold walks onstage with his tray as lights rise.

We hear street sounds.

Frank comes out of the shadows.

FRANK: You. You there. Come over here.

Harold looks around and then walks towards Frank. He realizes who it is.

FRANK: You got any matches?

Harold offers him a box of matches.

FRANK: How much?

Harold signals that they are free.

FRANK: Don't be ridiculous. You're a workingman. How much?

Harold holds up five fingers.

Frank reaches in his pocket and pulls out a quarter and flips it to Harold.

FARNK: Here's two bits. Keep the change.

Harold walks backwards away from Frank.

Frank lights a cigarette.

FRANK: Hey, wait a minute.

Harold stops.

Frank walks towards him.

FRANK: Were you around here last Thursday night, say about midnight?

Harold shakes his head no.

FRANK: 'Cause I have a friend that came to a bad end right here in this alley. You wouldn't know anything about that, would you?

Harold shakes his head again.

FRANK: Something wrong with you, pal?

Harold points to the sign on his tray.

FRANK: Hey, sorry about that. I didn't know. Must be hell trying to order a cup of coffee.

Harold shakes his head yes.

FRANK: But your eyesight is all right, yeah?

Harold shakes his head yes.

FRANK: And you can hear okay?

Harold nods yes.

FRANK: That's good. That's good. What God takes away he makes up in spades. Ain't that right?

Harold nods.

FRANK: That must mean you can hear and see better 'cause you can't talk.

Harold shrugs his shoulders.

FRANK: You must be able to see real good. Like things far away and in the shadows. You see probably better than a hawk. I bet you can hear real good, too. Like a dog. Making out words the rest of us can't even hear.

Frank takes another drag.

FRANK: Still, not being able to talk.

Frank drops his cigarette and steps on it.

FRANK: That must be rough.

Frank reaches into his jacket.

Harold backs away.

Frank takes out a flask and opens it to drink.

FRANK: We're getting a cold one tonight. You want a slug?

Harold waves his hands no.

Frank takes a drink and then puts the flask back in his jacket.

FRANK: You take care of yourself, pally. Keep your chin up, things will turn around for ya.

Frank walks offstage.

Harold falls to his knees when Frank is out of sight.

Dash comes in and sees Harold on the ground. He runs to him.

DASH: You okay, Newcomb? What happened?

Harold scratches a note and gives it to Dash.

DASH: Frank was here?

Harold writes.

DASH: He didn't know who you were. When was he here?

Harold holds up two fingers.

DASH: A couple of minutes ago? Which way did he go?

Harold points offstage.

DASH: You all right?

Harold nods yes.

DASH: Here's what I want you to do.

He helps Harold stand.

DASH: I want you to go over to the corner of Carson and Alameda, there's a precinct house. Get a hold of Detective Matthews in Homicide and tell him where you saw Frank.

Harold scratches a note.

DASH: I'm going after the rat that iced Joey and Kitten. Get to the precinct house and tell Matthews.

Harold writes.

DASH: Don't worry. He's running scared. And when you're scared, that's when you get caught.

Dash goes off in the same direction that Frank went.

Harold hurries off the other way.

Lights fade.

Lights come up dimly.

Dash is walking slowly across the stage with his gun pointed in front of him.

He stops and looks around.

Frank comes in from the shadows.

FRANK: That's far enough, Morgan. Drop the piece, and put your hands up.

DASH: Frank Banning. There's a lot of people looking for you, Frank. Why don't you make it easy on yourself and give up.

FRANK: There ain't nobody looking for me. I ain't done nothing.

DASH: Then why you pulling a gun, Frank?

FRANK: Let's call it insurance. Walk over this way.

Dash moves towards Frank.

DASH: The whole twelfth precinct is going to be coming around the corner in a minute, Frank. Why don't you just put down the gun and go quietly.

FRANK: I ain't never done nothing quietly, and I ain't about to start. Now tell me what Kitten was saying to you at the bar the other night?

DASH: How do you know about me talking to Kitten?

FRANK: I got my ways. What was she saying?

DASH: Kitten loved you, Frank. She wouldn't tell me anything. She kept her mouth shut like you told her to.

FRANK: Then why are you tailing me?

DASH: Remember the mute guy in the alley next to the Tick-Tock you just saw?

FRANK: Yeah, so what of it?

DASH: He saw the whole thing. He saw you kill Joey Numbers, and he came to me, 'cause the cops wouldn't listen. He saw the whole thing, and he wrote it all out. I got the statement back at the office just waiting for them to put the cuffs on you. That, plus the dying confession of Kitten Malone setting you up for her murder will likely put you in the electric chair before Christmas.

FRANK: I'm not going down without a fight, Morgan, and I'll take you with me if I have to.

DASH: It ain't going to be pretty, Frank. The cops don't like murderers walking the street.

FRANK: The cops can go to...

There is the sound of a toy horn being blown.

FRANK: What the?

Frank takes his eyes off of Dash towards the sound.

Dash pulls another gun from his jacket and fires at Frank.

Frank is shot and crumples to the ground.

Dash kicks his gun away from him.

Harold walks in from the shadows with the toy horn in his hand.

DASH: I was hoping that was you and not the circus in town. Did you get Matthews?

Harold nods.

DASH: I'd better check him and make sure he's not got another gun. You can never be too sure.

Dash bends down and searches through Frank's coat.

We hear sirens.

Harold turns and walks in the direction of the sirens looking away from the body.

Dash finds the brown paper package of money and stashes it in his own coat.

Detective Matthews enters.

DETECTIVE MATTHEWS: What we got here, Morgan?

DASH: Frank Banning, small time hood that tried to make it big but didn't make it past a dirty alley and a 38 slug. Here's his wallet and gun.

DETECTIVE MATTHEWS: Find anything else on him?

DASH: Nah, just that.

DETECTIVE MATTHEWS: Strange.

DASH: What's strange?

DETECTIVE MATTHEWS: Word on the street is that Joey Numbers was carrying about three grand the night that Frank killed him. The money's disappeared. You wouldn't know anything about that, would you, Morgan?

DASH: Come on, Matthews. I'm a law-abiding citizen.

DETECTIVE MATTHEWS: Sure you are, Morgan. Sure you are.

Matthews turns to Harold.

DETECTIVE MATTHEWS: I'm going to need you to come to the precinct and make a statement.

He turns back to Dash.

DETECTIVE MATTHEWS: You, too, Morgan.

DASH: You go on, Harold. I'll be right behind.

Detective Matthews exits with Harold.

Dash waits until they are gone and then takes the bundle from his jacket and flips through the bills.

DASH: Three thousand. That ought to be just about right.

He puts the bundle back in his jacket and goes off.

Lights fade.

Lights come up.

A box wrapped in Christmas paper with a visible tag saying "To Harold Newcomb" appears onstage.

Harold walks in with his tray around his neck and sees the box.

He bends down and picks it up and then opens it.

He takes out the bundle of cash and a note.

Dash appears off to the side to voice the note.

Harold reads.

DASH: Dear Harold. I told you I didn't do charity cases. Since this money would have just wound up in the precinct lockup, I figured it could be better used helping you out. So take it and go. Get out of this town. Go find yourself someplace quiet with trees where you can enjoy life. You were dealt a bum deal, Harold. Let's call this a new deck where all the cards are aces.

Harold looks at the money. He takes the tray off and sits it down on the ground with the sign facing out.

Harold exits.

Dash walks to center.

DASH: There's nothing like giving away three grand to make a guy feel hungry.

He takes out a quarter from his pocket and flips it in the air and catches it.

DASH: Heads.

He uncovers the coin.

DASH: I got to get another quarter. I think this one is broke.

Lights out.

Frank (Art Oden) and Kitten (Sarah Kelly) hover over the lifeless body of Joey Numbers (Michael C. Silva). Cinematography by Van Urfalian

Dash (Adam Hunter Howard) questions the validity of Harold's (Andrew J. Hillis) story. Cinematography by Van Urfalian

Dash (Adam Hunter Howard) prepares to interrogate Kitten (Sarah Kelly). Cinematography by Van Urfalian.

Frank (Art Oden) interrogates Harold (Andrew J. Hillis) during an investigation of his own. Cinematography by Van Urfalian.

Desperate Desires
By David Galanter

Desperate Desires by David Galanter. Copyright © 2013 by David Galanter. All rights reserved. Reprinted by permission of the author.

CAUTION/ADVICE Professionals and amateurs are hereby warned that performance of this play is subject to a royalty. It is fully protected under the copyright laws of the United States of America, and of all countries covered by the International Copyright Union (including the Dominion of Canada and the rest of the British Commonwealth), and of all countries covered by the Pan-American Copyright Convention and the Universal Copyright Convention, the Berne Convention, and of all countries with which the United States has reciprocal copyright relations. All rights, including professional and amateur stage performing rights, motion picture, recitation, lecturing, public reading, radio broadcasting, television, video or sound recording, all other forms of mechanical or electronic reproduction, such as CD-ROM, DVD-ROM, information storage or retrieval systems, and photocopying, and the rights of translation into foreign languages, are strictly reserved.

All inquiries concerning rights should be addressed to Punk Monkey Productions via email at info@punkmonkeyproductions.com.

David Galanter

David Galanter has been writing plays since he was a teenager and received his first publication at 18 years old for the one-act play *Concealed*. Years later he went on to write two 1940's, one-act comedies, *Desperate Desires* and *Wild Cards*, for PL.A.Y Noir's 2013 and 2015 seasons respectively. David also worked as an actor in L.A. for several years performing for thousand-person audiences for the Independent Shakespeare Company's 2010 and 2011 seasons in such plays as *Othello*, *Much Ado About Nothing*, and *Two Gentleman of Verona*. Obsessed with technology as well as classical entertainment, David eventual pursued a career in computer science and is currently a programmer at Psyonix, Inc. in San Diego working on the hit game *Rocket League*. See some of his work at: davidsportfolio.com.

Desperate Desires was originally produced by Punk Monkey Productions at the Actors Workout Studio in the North Hollywood Arts District in April 2013. It was directed by James Elden. The lighting design was by Shaunessy Quinn. The cast was as follows:

Cary Bogart..Jim Shipley
Virginia Hammers....................................Anna Laura Singleton

CHARACTERS:

> **CARY BOGART:** A conceded, 40-something year-old, 1940s private detective with the drive to solve any crime as long as it's safe and lucrative.
>
> **VIRGINIA HAMMERS:** A desperate, 30-something year-old client willing to part with her grand family fortune just to find her husband.
>
> *The sound of a lonely trumpet plays in the background. CARY BOGART stands by his window looking onto the city below in a loosened tie and suspenders, smoking a cigarette. His desk and chalkboard are covered with the details of countless crimes reported to his office.*

BOGART: *(Narration voice-over.)* There I was. January, 1941. Another night on another grind in the same town, The City of Angels. Yeah, right. The place is full of scum that keeps people like me in business. Robbers. Murderers. Dry Cleaners. Filthy bastards can't go five minutes without seeing some poor innocent victim suffer, and the robbers and murderers are even worse. They're all looking for a way to escape the righteous hands of justice my wrists have had the pleasure of accompanying for the past 20 years.

Knock at the door.

BOGART: *(V.O.)* There was a knock at the door. I had never ordered a pizza to the office before and wouldn't be stupid enough to start without a coupon. Gotta be careful in my line of work. Was it the mob unhappy with one of their thugs I put away? Or had I been working so hard I forgot to pay the rent? There's a million people it could have been, all worth talking about in endless details, but by now, I'm sure they were wondering what the hell was taking me so long. I could have thought of an excuse but decided to keep it simple.

BOGART: Mob or pizza?

HAMMERS: *(Offstage.)* What?

BOGART: *(V.O.)* Were they playing dumb? A heart of danger and the monotony of all this work inspired me to find out.

BOGART: Come in.

HAMMERS enters sporting a dazzling dress and purse, blatantly showing off her social status.

BOGART: *(V.O.)* There she was. The girl I'd never seen before. I could tell by the way she opened that door on command she listens attentively and is willing to cooperate. My kind of gal.

BOGART: Have a seat.

HAMMERS: No, thank you. I shouldn't stay long.

BOGART: *(V.O.)* Cold. Seems everything I'd come to know about this one was quickly going by the wayside. Either I was getting sluggish or she was a master of deception.

BOGART puts out his cigarette and walks towards HAMMERS.

BOGART: What's your name, doll?

HAMMERS: Hammers. Virginia Hammers.

BOGART: That's a beautiful name.

He takes her hand and tries to kiss it, while HAMMERS looks very uncomfortable. She pulls her hand away right after BOGART steals a smooch and smiles to save face.

BOGART: My name's Cary Bogart.

HAMMERS: I know. It's on your door.

BOGART: *(V.O.)* Strike two, toots. A detective can only be sassed so many times.

BOGART: So, what can I do for you, Miss Hammers?

HAMMERS: I'd like to report a missing person. It's my husband.

BOGART: *(V.O.)* I knew it. Despite all the obvious advancements she had been making, she was married. Is nothing sacred anymore?

BOGART: Husband, huh? What's his name?

HAMMERS: Walter Krivitsky.

BOGART: Different last name?

HAMMERS looks somewhat uncomfortable from the question and takes it upon herself to sit down. BOGART looks annoyed.

HAMMERS: The marriage was something of a secret. My safety might have been in jeopardy considering his profession at the time.

BOGART: And what profession was that? *(HAMMERS seems uneasy.)* If you want help, I gotta know what you know.

HAMMERS: Aren't you going to offer me a drink first?

BOGART: Nice try. Aiming to smear a good detective's name with illegal substances, are we? Everyone in this office obeys the law, including prohibition.

HAMMERS: Prohibition's been dead for almost ten years now.

BOGART: *(V.O.)* I knew I shouldn't have stopped buying newspapers to save money. Sure did help me afford all this booze, I will say that much.

BOGART opens his idyllic cabinet full of booze.

BOGART: Scotch okay?

HAMMERS: Anything.

BOGART starts pouring drinks for the both of them.

BOGART: You a resident?

HAMMERS: *(Still hesitant having not gotten her drink.)* This city is my home, but it seems like I'm never here.

BOGART: Sounds nice. Unfortunately, I rarely get a chance to travel anywhere outside this office.

HAMMERS: I'd spend a thousand years in one spot if it meant finding my husband.

BOGART: *(V.O.)* I could have set her straight and told her how useless such a deal would be without the lifespan to back it up, but she was desperate, and it didn't take a fashion expert to tell she had money. It eased the pain pouring my ten-dollar Scotch down the drain knowing one case with her could keep me in business for months. Yeah, a whole ten dollars.

He hands over HAMMER'S glass of Scotch.

BOGART: Tell me about him.

HAMMERS: I can't say too much.

BOGART: *(V.O.)* No-good waste of quality liquor. If playing games was a game, she'd be a pro.

BOGART: You have to give me something if you want me to do my job.

HAMMERS: Try to understand, Mr. Bogart, I'm here because I know you'll take any case, no questions asked, for the right price.

BOGART: That depends if we agree on the definition of "right price." I don't have to do anything if I feel like it's not worth getting involved with whatever your husband did for a living.

HAMMERS: Please. I'll pay whatever you want. Others are looking for him, and I want to find him first. I want him safe.

BOGART: This is getting better and better by the minute. I have a short time table, little to no information, and it's all just to get in the way some of conflict I nothing to do with.

HAMMERS: But I was told you have a heart of danger.

BOGART: *(V.O.)* She was in my head faster than a psychic reading my thoughts...

BOGART looks at HAMMERS suspicious if she can hear his narration.

BOGART: *(V.O.)* Her awkward silence indicated that wasn't actually the case. I needed more but wasn't ready to lie down and roll over like some sort of dog.

BOGART: Listen, I'm havin' a ball, but you could have just contacted me on the Ameche. Then you wouldn't have wasted your time gammin' in here all ginned up like a Fifth Avenue duchess on her way to a frolic pad. Not to mention, the lettuce you wasted taking a barouche all the way downtown thinking you could bunny me into doing whatever you want. If I had known you were going to sling around a bunch of gobbledygook instead of real info, I might not have let your kicks in the door. *(Short pause.)* "Ball" means "good time."

HAMMERS: I know what "having a ball" means! I'm a very powerful woman. I can make it worth your while.

Next few lines delivered quickly.

BOGART: I don't care if you're Captain America-

HAMMERS: -Too late-

BOGART: -Robin-

HAMMERS: -Not relevant-

BOGART: -Superman-

HAMMERS: -Nailed it-

BOGART: -that doesn't mean you can waltz in here bragging about your fortune like some taxi driver who just saved a bunch of money on his car insurance by switching to Geico.

HAMMERS gives a look like she's about to point something out.

BOGART: They were founded in 1936. Give it a rest! Why can't you be more like Germany and take the law into your own hands?

HAMMERS: I tried to look for him on my own, but I need help.

BOGART: What if I refuse?

HAMMERS: I'm begging you.

HAMMERS gets up and moves in closer to BOGART.

HAMMERS: I can't tell you how much this means to me.

BOGART leans in fast and kisses HAMMERS. The following narration plays over their kiss as HAMMERS squirms, looking confused and disgusted.*

BOGART: *(V.O.)* We both couldn't deny it any longer. She wanted me, and I wasn't about to resist. Her complete disregard for her husband made me sick, appalled, and aroused all at the same time. Who knew how many guys she had been with while his life was in danger. Some people are so desperate it tears me up inside.

HAMMERS pulls away shocked and angry.

BOGART: *(V.O.)* She slapped me.

HAMMERS slaps him.

BOGART: *(V.O.)* Twice.

HAMMERS slaps him again.

BOGART: *(V.O.)* And I can't remember if she kneed me in the groin.

HAMMERS knees him in the groin.

BOGART: *(V.O.)* She did.

Bogart acts on cue with the descriptions in the following voice-over but projects a lot more pain in his actions than he's admitting to in his narration.

BOGART: *(V.O.)* I played it cool and stood up tall to let her know what kind of a man she was dealing with, until a very small amount of discomfort started creeping up into my stomach, forcing me to hunch over slightly. She stood her ground, mad as a cow with a disease, as I wiped the water from my eyes. It was definitely dry in there or something. I sat down on my own accord to let her know I was done with our little love affair. What little pain there was completely disappeared, as I laid my head on the desk bored of her interest in me. After I felt she had enough punishment, I did her the favor of hearing more of what she had to say.

BOGART's head remains on the desk, clearly still in pain.

BOGART: Go on.

HAMMERS: My husband is not an American but has been hiding out in the states for quite some time. He usually keeps in touch with me, but he mentioned the people looking for him might be close. I haven't been able to reach him after that. L.A. was the last place I heard from him, and that's all I can reveal. I'll pay more than enough to compensate for sparse details. *(Short pause.)* Can you hear me?

BOGART: Yeah, yeah, I hear you. *(He lifts his head from the desk.)* You're rich. I heard you the first ten times, and I don't think I'm interested in hearing it again. Furthermore, I've heard enough to know this case doesn't sound like my cup of tea. Sorry you wasted your time, but I can't help you. Have a good day, Miss Hammers. You can keep the drink.

BOGART gets up and turns around to put away the liquor bottle while HAMMERS pulls out a revolver and points it at him with his back still turned.

BOGART: *(V.O.)* I had to let her down hard, only way to get the idea of the two of us out of her head for good. Right then I was certain she was crying, knowing she had to crawl back to her husband she can't even find. I almost didn't want to turn around fearing she'd try imposing her emotions on me as if they were my problem…

BOGART turns around and sees the gun.

BOGART: *(V.O.)* With a gun. She held the grip firmly in one hand, and I was pretty sure the dangerous end was pointed right at me. Some people just don't know how to deal with heartbreak.

BOGART: What's that for? Killing me isn't going to help you get over our little fling any faster.

HAMMERS: I don't want you. I want Krivitsky.

BOGART: Your husband's your own problem, sweetheart.

HAMMERS: He's not my husband, you imbecile. He was a spy for the Soviet Union that defected recently, and my employers have been looking to silence him for a very long time. I was told to use any means necessary to track him down.

BOGART: If you think I'm gonna do this job at gunpoint, you're in for a disappoint.

HAMMERS: You don't get to do this job anymore. You know too much. You should have taken the money.

BOGART: You probably would have buried me with him in the end anyway.

HAMMERS: Doesn't matter now.

BOGART: Calm down. You don't really want to pull that trigger.

She shoots the ground near his feet.

BOGART: *(V.O.)* I knew she wanted to pull that trigger. Reverse psychology was never my strong suit

BOGART: I don't know anything. Hammers probably isn't even your real name. All I know is there's a man out there with an expiration date on his get-out-of-bullet-wounds-free card. That's half the sorry saps walking around this town. Welcome to L.A. I was wrong. You are like Germany. Determined to get what you want, when you want, in your glorious attempt to do what needs to be done. Like America itself, I respect that and feel no responsibility to stop you. Walk out that door. Your real target awaits and you know I'm not worth the hassle.

HAMMERS backs slowly off stage making sure never to take the gun off BOGART. She exits.

BOGART: *(V.O.)* And just like that it was over. Poor bastard was found dead a month later. The papers I started buying again claimed suicide. I wasn't about to testify. I'm here and he's not, and there's no good reason why.

BOGART walks back to look out the window.

BOGART: *(V.O.)* The City of Angels. I just might get these pants dry-cleaned.

End.

Stiff
By Hope Thompson

Stiff by Hope Thompson. Copyright © 2013 by Hope Thompson. All rights reserved. Reprinted by permission of the author.

CAUTION/ADVICE Professionals and amateurs are hereby warned that performance of this play is subject to a royalty. It is fully protected under the copyright laws of the United States of America, and of all countries covered by the International Copyright Union (including the Dominion of Canada and the rest of the British Commonwealth), and of all countries covered by the Pan-American Copyright Convention and the Universal Copyright Convention, the Berne Convention, and of all countries with which the United States has reciprocal copyright relations. All rights, including professional and amateur stage performing rights, motion picture, recitation, lecturing, public reading, radio broadcasting, television, video or sound recording, all other forms of mechanical or electronic reproduction, such as CD-ROM, DVD-ROM, information storage or retrieval systems, and photocopying, and the rights of translation into foreign languages, are strictly reserved.

All inquiries concerning rights should be addressed to Punk Monkey Productions via email at info@punkmonkeyproductions.com.

Hope Thompson

Hope is a Canadian playwright, filmmaker and crime writer. She is interested in mystery, film noir, camp and comedy and has written and directed several award-winning short films and one-act plays in these genres. Hope's monologue, *Cardigan Confidential* was published in the collection, *City Voices: A Book of Monologues by Toronto Artists* and she performed it at World Pride in Toronto in 2014. www.hopethompson.net

Stiff was originally produced by Punk Monkey Productions under the title *Outside Job* at the Actors Workout Studio in the North Hollywood Arts District in April 2013. It was directed by Sarah Kelly. The lighting design was by Shaunessy Quinn. The cast was as follows:

Leyland	Christopher Flowers
Isabelle	Elisa Dyann
Bob	Michael C. Silva
Carol	Rebecca Herrick

The first production under the title *Stiff* was at Buddies in Bad Times Theatre in Toronto, Canada as part of the triple-bill, *Fear and Desire (and the whole damn thing)*, November 29-December 1, 2013. It was directed by Clinton Walker. The cast was as follows:

Leyland	Greg Campbell
Isabelle	Mary Krohnert
Bob	Andy Pogson
Carol	Kirsten Johnson

CHARACTERS:

LEYLAND
ISABELLE
BOB
CAROL

The year is 1953. The location is a dark, wood-paneled room with a sofa and two chairs.

The room has one door and one window. There is a baronial quality to this room.

Gathered here are two couples: Bob and Carol & Leyland and Isabelle.

There is one window. Police are stationed outside.

BOB paces near the window, glancing out occasionally.

CAROL sits on the couch, knitting—sharp needles clicking.

LEYLAND sits in a chair reading a newspaper.

ISABELLE sits in the other chair breathing rapidly, about to explode.

A tense, long silence...

ISABELLE: I am sick of this! He has no right to keep us locked up here like common criminals!

BOB: But we are criminals. I mean one of us is.

CAROL: Oh, shush, Bob. You're just making things worse. Isabelle's right. We're not criminals. The whole thing's a misunderstanding. Just as soon as that fool of a detective gets things sorted out, we can get on our way home.

Carol frowns at her knitting project.

CAROL: Obviously it was an outside job.

BOB: Carol, honey, this is not some cheap paperback mystery. We're on the hook for murder here. I mean, one of us is—

CAROL: Oh, for goodness sake, will you give it a rest? And whose bright idea was it to come up here, anyway?

Carol shoots a glance at Leyland.

BOB: Crenshaw's an old friend. Why, he goes back to our college days. Right, Leyland?

Leyland grunts from behind his newspaper.

BOB: And when an old friend invites you for a weekend, you can't very well turn him down, now can you?

Bob stops and thinks.

BOB: Course if we had, we wouldn't be on the hook for murder. I mean, one of us.

ISABELLE: *(Grabbing at tissues from her purse.)* I can't bear it! I simply cannot bear it. I'll go crazy. I will quite literally go crazy—

CAROL: Bob, will you stop upsetting Isabelle?

BOB: I'm sorry, Isabelle, but you're just going to have to pull yourself together. Crenshaw's dead, and one of us killed him. We're the only people here, so it's got to be one of us. Why, his body's lying in the hallway right now with a huge knife sticking out of it. Well, more of a sword, really. Right honey?

Carol ignores him and keeps on knitting.

ISABELLE: *(Recoiling, covering her mouth.)* Oh, dear God.

LEYLAND: *(Looking up from his newspaper.)* You're positively enjoying this, aren't you, Bob? Which one of us did it? You? Me? Maybe it was the two girls together? You never can trust a skirt once your back's turned.

ISABELLE: Oh, Leyland...

Isabelle covers her face in her hands, trembling.

LEYLAND: *(Ignoring her.)* What about you, Bob? Where were you last night? Establishing an alibi?

CAROL: He was in bed with me.

BOB: That's right. I was. As Carol has told you.

Carol and Bob exchange looks.

LEYLAND: Must have been quite an active night if you're willing to vouch for Bob's presence at your side the entire night.

CAROL: It wasn't active at all. But he was there nonetheless.

LEYLAND: *(Leyland grins at Carol.)* I'm not surprised it wasn't active. Nonetheless.

ISABELLE: Leyland, this isn't funny—

LEYLAND: Am I laughing? Smirking, perhaps, but certainly not laughing.

Bob fidgets; anxious...

BOB: *(To Leyland.)* What about you? Where were you last night?

LEYLAND: Me? Why, I was roaming the halls. But first I went to the kitchen and took the carving knife from the drawer.

BOB: *(Eyes popping.)* The carving knife?

LEYLAND: For protection. I find Crenshaw's mansion quite unsettling, what with all the sets of armor and paintings of retched old ancestors staring out from every wall. Menacing sort of place, I've always thought.

Leyland leers at the group, brandishing an imaginary knife.

LEYLAND: But I had my knife, see?

ISABELLE: Then you— Oh, Leyland?

CAROL: He's only joking.

LEYLAND: Am I?

Leyland picks up his paper and continues reading.

The SOUND of a vehicle arriving.

Bob runs to the window and stares; lights play over his face.

BOB: *(Whistling in amazement.)* Here's the ambulance! They'll be collecting Crenshaw's body, I bet. Taking it to the morgue for an autopsy. Will you look at that? There's three fellas going inside with a stretcher. And a photographer, too. Holy-moly…

Bob stares out the window, lost in thought.

BOB: Poor Crenshaw. What a way to die. I wouldn't want to be stabbed. I imagine you'd feel a good deal of pain upon entry. Then bleed to death very slowly—

ISABELLE: STOP IT! Please!

BOB: Sorry.

LEYLAND: Poor Crenshaw— yes, but I won't miss the old—

BOB: *(Cutting off Leyland.)* —inveterate experimenter. Right, Leyland? Me and the other fellas just called him mad. Old Crenshaw, the mad professor. But I always liked how you used to say he was an inveterate—

CAROL: *(Cutting off Bob.)* Experimenter? What do you mean by that?

BOB: Well, you see he used to—

LEYLAND: *(Cutting off Bob; putting down his paper and standing up.)* Crenshaw was always looking for cures. Insomnia, vertigo, public speaking, you name it; he was on the case to solve it. He had shelves of every potion imaginable and every one of them registered with the patent office. But for all that, I've never known any of his cures to actually work.

BOB: *(Nodding vigorously.)* Yeah, yeah. Crazy stuff. Vertigo, you name it—

LEYLAND: *(Cutting off Bob.)* But the real problem with Crenshaw, I've always thought, is that he tested his experiments on himself. That the man was gravely ill, I've no doubt. I mean, just think of that skin condition he had. His skin was practically, well— dripping.

BOB: *(Grinning.)* His skin made my skin crawl.

ISABELLE: *(Covering her mouth, about to be sick.)* Oh god—

LEYLAND: *(Putting his arm around her.)* Darling, what is it?

ISABELLE: *(Pulling away.)* Don't touch me!

Leyland frowns.

LEYLAND: At any rate, he spent his whole life experimenting. Trying to achieve immortality, I suppose. That must be why one does these things. To have one's name remembered, after death, as it were.

Isabelle fidgets, knuckles raw and tense.

ISABELLE: Well, it didn't work, did it? He's forgotten.

LEYLAND: Darling?

ISABELLE: You heard me!

LEYLAND: Are you sure you're all right?

ISABELLE: Oh, I'm fine, Leyland. Just fine.

Bob and Carol stare at them. Leyland clears his throat, uncomfortable.

An uneasy silence settles over the room.

BOB: Say! What about those pills Crenshaw mentioned at dinner last night? He seemed pretty excited. Maybe he was finally on to something, eh, Leyland? His big breakthrough, huh?

LEYLAND: *(Smirking.)* You mean his pleasure pill? The dirty old man.

CAROL: *(Alarmed.)* What pill? What are you talking about?

BOB: Heck, it's hard to describe. Isn't it, Leyland?

LEYLAND: *(Cutting him off.)* Pleasure, Carol! We're talking about pleasure.

CAROL: Oh.

LEYLAND: It's a 'men-only' matter.

CAROL: I see. But what's it got to do with Crenshaw?

BOB: The pleasure pill is one of his inventions. He mentioned it last night. Went on and on about it. Don't you remember?

CAROL: *(Returning to her knitting.)* No. I don't. I must have blocked it out. Crenshaw? Really? At his age?

BOB: I know. It's amazing.

CAROL: It's disgusting is what it is.

Leyland sits down beside Isabelle.

LEYLAND: It doesn't work, so you needn't be offended.

CAROL: *(To Leyland.)* How do you know it doesn't work?

BOB: Weren't you listening, honey? All Crenshaw's cures failed. Leyland here just explained that a minute ago. None of his cures have ever worked.

LEYLAND: A pity, too.

BOB: *(Nodding.)* I'll say.

CAROL: You men are depraved, you hear me? Depraved. I don't understand why you can't just—read books! Just read a good book. I mean, why keep pestering us night after night? Why? Why?

ISABELLE: They're animals. That's why!

Everyone turns and stares at Isabelle, surprised.

LEYLAND: We men desire the feminine sex from time to time. Don't we, Bob?

BOB: Huh? Oh, yeah, yeah, sure.

ISABELLE: Do you, Leyland? Really? It's been some time.

Leyland picks up his newspaper and reads.

BOB: Carol's always been a great reader, haven't you, dear? She reads and re-reads the Classics, don't you, dear? That private girls school you ladies went to really paid off. You've got the reading bug, all right. Why she even reads while we—

CAROL: Are you finished?

BOB: Huh?

CAROL: We acquired many things at Grandhurst besides a love of the Classics. Didn't we, Isabelle?

ISABELLE: I don't remember. It was years ago.

CAROL: Sometimes it seems like just yesterday.

Carol and Isabelle exchange glances.

Isabelle looks away.

SOUNDs of doors shutting, men's indistinct voices—Bob runs to the window.

BOB: *(Whistles in amazement.)* Holy cow.

CAROL: What? What is it now?

BOB: They're taking him away. Crenshaw. He's on a stretcher covered in a white sheet. I mean I think that's him. What do you know? I've never seen a stiff in real life...

LEYLAND: *(Making a joke)* I'm not surprised.

No one laughs.

Bob turns from the window to the group.

BOB: *(To the group.)* Hey, you know what this means?

CAROL: That you've had a new experience seeing your first corpse?

BOB: No. I mean, yes, but that's not what I was thinking of—

ISABELLE: Well what then? What does it mean, Bob?

BOB: It means that detective will be coming to get our statements. What else does he have to do now but get our statements, now that Crenshaw's body's been removed from the scene of the—crime? Oh no...

Bob sits down, lost.

BOB: What do we tell him, Carol? What do we say?

CAROL: We tell the truth.

LEYLAND: *(Looking up from his paper, grinning.)* So you weren't at your wife's side all night, after all.

CAROL: He was.

BOB: Yes, I was. Well, for most of the night.

CAROL: Bob?

BOB: But you said to tell the truth?

Carol knits vigorously.

LEYLAND: Now, this is getting interesting. Well? Out with it. Are you the killer, Bob? I might have known.

CAROL: Oh, Leyland, stop it!

LEYLAND: No need to get testy. *(Turning to Bob, smiling.)* Well? What were you doing last night when you weren't snuggled up next to Carol?

BOB: *(Hesitating.)* Well... I was thirsty. I went looking for a glass of water, that's all. Oh, and to use the facilities. That's when I heard the talking in your room.

LEYLAND: Talking?

BOB: Voices. I couldn't make out what was being said. Maybe I shouldn't have mentioned—

LEYLAND: What voices, Bob?

BOB: Oh, I don't know. Just my ears playing tricks— most likely.

CAROL: Yes, most likely that was it.

ISABELLE: These old houses do tend to echo, don't they?

(Leyland stares at Isabelle and Carol.)

LEYLAND: *(Carefully.)* I must have been talking in my sleep.

BOB: Except I'm pretty sure it wasn't your voice I heard—

ISABELLE: Oh, where is that detective? Are we going to be kept locked up here forever?

LEYLAND: *(Smirking.)* If it wasn't me, then who was it, Bob? Crenshaw?

Leyland laughs.

BOB: Why, yes, actually.

Leyland looks around, confused.

LEYLAND: Crenshaw? But— what would he be doing—

Leyland turns to Isabelle.

LEYLAND: In my room?

Isabelle turns away from him.

BOB: Hey?

LEYLAND: *(Grabbing Bob's shirt collar.)* Now, you look here. I don't know what you heard, but it wasn't Crenshaw. You understand me?

BOB: I'm telling the truth! I heard him in your room. He was banging around—

LEYLAND: He was what?

Leyland peers over his shoulder at Isabelle then back to Bob.

BOB: I said he was banging—

LEYLAND: You want to know what it feels like to be stabbed? If I had a knife, I'd sink it into your ribs this minute—

BOB: But I don't understand. Surely you saw him. I mean he was *in your room* for goodness sake.

Leyland releases Bob from his grip and walks away from the group. He stares out the window.

BOB: *(Brushing himself off, muttering.)* What's the big idea, anyway?

ISABELLE: Look, Bob, Leyland and I— well, I may as well tell you—

LEYLAND: You may as well not!

ISABELLE: Oh, what's the difference?

LEYLAND: I would prefer that you didn't—

ISABELLE: *(Cutting Leyland off.)* We slept in separate rooms last night! As we do every night. Which is why Leyland didn't hear—

LEYLAND: That's quite enough!

ISABELLE: Stop acting like a child. It's nothing to be ashamed of.

Carol laughs, low and long.

LEYLAND: *(Turning to Carol.)* You're the one who ought to be ashamed.

BOB: Now, you wait a minute—

LEYLAND: *(Ignoring Bob.)* You never got over Grandhurst and all those close, close female friendships, did you? I've seen you looking at Isabelle. Desperate. That's what you are: desperate and pathetic.

BOB: You listen here, Leyland—

ISABELLE: *(Angry.)* Don't you talk to Carol like that. She—

Isabelle breaks down.

BOB: Isabelle, what is it? Look, would someone tell me what's going on here? What are you insinuating about my wife? And what in Heaven's name was Crenshaw doing in your room?

ISABELLE: I can't say it.

LEYLAND: *(Warning.)* There's nothing to say. Crenshaw was never in— our room.

Carol stops knitting.

ISABELLE: *(Through tears.)* But he was. He was!

Silence; everyone stares at Isabelle.

ISABELLE: I heard footsteps. In the hallway. Getting louder. Coming closer. They wakened me.

She fusses with a tissue.

ISABELLE: I was scared. I— I don't know why. It could have been anyone walking past the door, but for some reason, it frightened me. The footsteps were so loud. Pounding in my head.

LEYLAND: Isabelle...

ISABELLE: Then the— the doorknob began to turn. I could hardly breathe. It rotated round and round and round. Then pushed in.

(She collects herself, breathing hard.)

ISABELLE: He was standing there: a figure in the doorway. I didn't know who it was at first. The light from the hallway was behind him. His face was in darkness... but it was clear what he was after.

LEYLAND: *(Astonished.)* Crenshaw?

ISABELLE: Yes! Him!

LEYLAND: But it's impossible.

ISABELLE: Leyland his skin was on me! His horrible, dripping skin. I— I thought I would die.

She shivers, rocking back and forth.

LEYLAND: Darling...

ISABELLE: Don't touch me!

LEYLAND: Look, darling—

Isabelle shrinks away.

Silence.

BOB: Say, I wonder if he was testing that pleasure pill of his.

ISABELLE: Well, it works. By God, it works!

Leyland stands up, pacing, thinking.

LEYLAND: Funny.

ISABELLE: Funny?

LEYLAND: Well, yes, you see I took one, too. One of Crenshaw's pleasure pills.

BOB: But I thought you said he only tested his experiments on himself?

LEYLAND: Yes, but I, well, I asked to try one. After he told us about the pleasure pill, I went to him. After everyone had gone to bed. I begged him to let me try it.

ISABELLE: Then why weren't you with me, in my bed?

LEYLAND: Well, I, I thought I'd wait until it worked, then come to you in the night.

CAROL: Just like Crenshaw? How romantic.

LEYLAND: Darling, please—

BOB: Say, Leyland, did it work? The pill, I mean?

LEYLAND: What? Oh, no. I swallowed it, but nothing happened. I mean, I awoke when I heard the commotion. When Crenshaw's body was found. I slept through the whole thing. Rather soundly, as a matter of fact.

Leyland sits down beside Isabelle and clasps her hands.

LEYLAND: Isabelle, darling, I never dreamed he'd try to... Look, we'll get through this.

ISABELLE: *(Breaking down.)* I'm frightened. I'm frightened.

LEYLAND: Don't worry. We'll fight this thing. It was simply an act of self-defense. We'll get you off. You'll see. Why, we'll get you the best lawyer in town—

BOB: *(Looking out the window and whistling in amazement.)* He better be the best lawyer in the state.

CAROL: Why? What is it?

BOB: He's going up against the D. A. himself.

LEYLAND: The District Attorney? You're kidding.

BOB: I wish I was. He just got out of a car with a couple of other fellas. Holy Dinah, this is serious.

Bob spins away from the window.

BOB: Isabelle? The D. A.'s going to convict you of— murder.

Isabelle covers her face.

CAROL: No, he's not.

BOB: Huh?

CAROL: I said, no, he's not.

BOB: Why, you mean, not if Isabelle's lawyer manages to persuade the jury otherwise—

CAROL: Isabelle didn't do it. That's what I mean.

Bob stares at Carol, confused.

BOB: Pardon?

ISABELLE: Carol, please—

CAROL: I did it.

BOB: You?

CAROL: Yes. I went to Isabelle's room last night, but when I got to her door, I heard, well, unusual sounds coming from inside. I thought— something is wrong. I— I pushed opened the door and— entered. That's when I saw him. Crenshaw. That disgusting old man and his desperate, craving body— *(To Isabelle.)* I couldn't bear it. I couldn't bear to see him—with you.

She covers her mouth.

CAROL: I— I took the sword from that old set of armor in the hallway. I crept up behind him— and I— I plunged the blade into his body just as hard as I could.

Isabelle gasps.

CAROL: I dragged him into the hallway— I tried to make it look like— an outside job.

Carol winds wool into a ball.

BOB: *(Whispering.)* You— killed Crenshaw?

CAROL: Yes! I killed him. And I'd kill him again and again and again if I could.

The others stare at her, stunned.

BOB: *(Swallowing.)* Carol?

CAROL: You heard me.

LEYLAND: *(Relaxing.)* Well, well, well. Interesting. But not surprising. Inversion knows no bounds.

A light bulb turns on in Leyland's head.

LEYLAND: *(To Isabelle.)* Wait a minute. What was she doing sneaking into your— I mean, our— room?

ISABELLE: What does it matter? Carol saved me, Leyland. She saved me while you were sleeping.

LEYLAND: So she could have her way with you. She's the one that's caused my problems, I'll bet. Her and all that Grandhurst business—

BOB: Now, hold your horses, Leyland—

ISABELLE: That's not true. It's simply not true.

LEYLAND: It is true. And I for one won't be sad to see her behind bars.

ISABELLE: Oh, Leyland. You don't understand.

LEYLAND: I understand only too well. Right beneath my nose. How do you like that?

CAROL: *(To Leyland.)* You understand nothing, and you never have.

LEYLAND: *(Lunging at Carol, struggling with her.)* What did you say?

ISABELLE: *(Pulling Carol off Leyland.)* She's right!

LEYLAND: *(Struggling with Carol.)* She's right? She's never been right since the day she was born—

BOB: *(Pulling Leyland off Carol.)* Okay, that does it—

ISABELLE: Stop it, Leyland. Stop it! You're acting like a child.

Bob and Isabelle pull Carol and Leyland apart.

CAROL: *(Brushing herself off.)* I suppose one does when one can no longer function like a man.

LEYLAND: *(Prepares to punch Carol.)* Why I ought to—

Bob grabs Leyland's arm and yanks it into an arm lock.

BOB: You ought to mind your manners is what you ought to do.

LEYLAND: *(Wincing.)* All right, all right—

Bob reluctantly releases Leyland.

CAROL: *(Sitting down.)* I'll bet that was a sleeping pill Crenshaw gave you.

LEYLAND: *(Straightening his jacket.)* That's ridiculous. He told me it was a pleasure pill. Why would he lie? He's an old friend and my former professor. I trust him completely.

ISABELLE: Leyland?!

LEYLAND: I meant I used to trust him.

CAROL: Which is why he knew he could manipulate you! You begged him for the pill. I bet he told you to sleep in your own room, didn't he? And to surprise Isabelle when you were—ready.

Carol shudders, disgusted.

CAROL: That's right, isn't it? Crenshaw knew you'd do exactly what he said.

LEYLAND: Well, yes— he did suggest that, but—

ISABELLE: *(Breaking down.)* Oh, Leyland, don't you see?

LEYLAND: But I— I didn't do anything wrong. I was just— just trying to make things better for us.

Leyland spins around, pointing at Carol.

LEYLAND: *(Pleading with Isabelle.)* It's her! She's trying to come between us. Putting words in my mouth. She's the real problem here.

BOB: *(Assertive.)* What was that?

ISABELLE: *(Pushing Leyland away.)* Enough.

Silence; they stare at each other.

CAROL: *(To Leyland.)* Look, I might as well tell you.

ISABELLE: Carol, don't—

Carol sets down her ball of wool.

CAROL: I have always loved your wife.

BOB: Huh?

CAROL: But she doesn't love me. Not in that way.

Turning to Isabelle.

CAROL: Perhaps you never did.

LEYLAND: Perhaps?

CAROL: Or maybe it was just a childhood infatuation...back in Grandhurst. But for me, it was love. It always has been. Love as I've never known it before.

BOB: Carol?

CAROL: Oh, Bob. Don't look so sad. There are so many different kinds of love, and we do have such big hearts, don't we?

Carol collects herself.

CAROL: I thought we might find a way back. To those days. Those feelings. Oh, I know it was foolish. But there's something about this awful place. These old, stone walls, they remind me of Grandhurst. I've been half blind with desire ever since I got here.

Bob recoils

CAROL: *(Laughing, embarrassed.)* My knitting's the only thing that keeps my mind off it. Oh, Isabelle, I'm sorry for pestering you. I really am.

Carol breaks down.

CAROL: But I'm not sorry about Crenshaw! I couldn't bear seeing you and him—together...

ISABELLE: Oh, Carol...don't cry.

LEYLAND: Save your tears for the judge.

ISABELLE: Leyland?

LEYLAND: She's a cold-blooded murderer is what she is.

CAROL: *(Cold, impenetrable.)* I'll hang for it. I don't care.

BOB: *(Rushing to Carol.)* Hang—? Now wait a minute here. Whatever this business is with Isabelle, it's in the past and that's where we're leaving it. But when you say you'll hang for it and that you don't care, why, you must care! You can't leave me, Carol. What will I do?

CAROL: You'll be all right.

BOB: Alone?

CAROL: You must be strong now.

Bob stares at her, confused.

Carol resumes winding wool into a ball.

Leyland leans back, hands behind his head.

LEYLAND: So, the truth comes out. And what a twisted tale it is. How do you like that? Of course, I was right all along.

Isabelle walks away from Leyland.

ISABELLE: You think of no one but yourself. You make it so hard to love you. Sometimes I wonder why I even bother.

LEYLAND: Now darling, that's not true at all—

Isabelle sits beside Carol.

ISABELLE: Carol... I do love you. I always have. And in the only way that, well, that really matters. Thank you for what you did.

Kissing Carol's cheek, embracing her.

ISABELLE: Thank you, from both of us. Right, Leyland?

LEYLAND: What? You expect me to thank her—

ISABELLE: CAROL SAVED ME!

LEYLAND: Well, all right. I— I should have been there to protect my wife. Thank you. I might add, though, that Isabelle and I will be sleeping in the same room from now on.

ISABELLE: Is that a threat?

LEYLAND: Darling, it is simply common sense. The pleasure pill obviously works, so why wouldn't we share the same bed?

ISABELLE: Pleasure... *Your pleasure...*

LEYLAND: Well, yours, too, I like to think.

Bob hears something. He runs to the door and puts his ear against it.

BOB: *(Whispering.)* Someone's coming. I bet it's the D.A.! What do we tell him? ...Carol?

Everyone looks at Carol.

CAROL: I don't want to die.

Carol breaks down.

Bob stares at the group, breathing hard, thinking fast. His face hardens.

BOB: You're not going to die. We're going to get out of this. Somehow.

Carol looks at Bob, blinking back tears.

CAROL: But, how?

BOB: What's going to link you to the murder? Come on, think! What happens in those cheap mysteries? Fingerprints! That's it. We'll clean the sword handle. Where is it?

CAROL: It's in the body.

LEYLAND: And the police have the body.

ISABELLE: Oh, it's no use. They'll find out you did it.

Isabelle sniffles.

BOB: There's got to be another way out of this.

LEYLAND: I doubt it.

ISABELLE: Her fingerprints are on the sword handle. It's impossible.

SOUND of footsteps in the distance.

CAROL: I wore mittens.

BOB: Mittens? But— where are they now?

CAROL: They're gone.

BOB: Gone where? Look this is no time for games—

SOUND of footsteps nearing, louder.

CAROL: They're gone. The mittens are gone.

Carol holds up the ball of wool.

CAROL: *(Wiping away tears.)* Unraveled. I'm starting over.

ISABELLE: Oh, Carol...

Leyland and Bob rush over to the women and stand behind them, forming a tight, defensive group.

BOB: *(Solemn.)* I swear Crenshaw's murder was an outside job.

Bob rests his hand on Carol's shoulder.

SOUND of footsteps LOUD, approaching the door.

ISABELLE: *(Clasping Carol's hands in hers.)* Yes, I agree completely! Leyland?

Isabelle looks up at Leyland, smiling.

Leyland rests his hand on her shoulder, smiling down at her.

LEYLAND: Yes, of course, my darling.

LOUD SOUND of a doorknob turning, round and round.

The group recoil in fear as the room falls into darkness.

ISABELLE: Carol? I'm starting over, too.

A shaft of light hits the group as the door pushes opens; the dark silhouette of a man fills the doorframe—his shadow spills over the group.

Carol turns to Isabelle.

Lights out.

END.

The Zone Ranger
By Ben Goldstein and Mac Taylor

The Zone Ranger by Ben Goldstein and Mac Taylor. Copyright © 2009 by Mac Taylor and Ben Goldstein. All rights reserved. Reprinted by permission of the authors.

CAUTION/ADVICE Professionals and amateurs are hereby warned that performance of this play is subject to a royalty. It is fully protected under the copyright laws of the United States of America, and of all countries covered by the International Copyright Union (including the Dominion of Canada and the rest of the British Commonwealth), and of all countries covered by the Pan-American Copyright Convention and the Universal Copyright Convention, the Berne Convention, and of all countries with which the United States has reciprocal copyright relations. All rights, including professional and amateur stage performing rights, motion picture, recitation, lecturing, public reading, radio broadcasting, television, video or sound recording, all other forms of mechanical or electronic reproduction, such as CD-ROM, DVD-ROM, information storage or retrieval systems, and photocopying, and the rights of translation into foreign languages, are strictly reserved.

All inquiries concerning rights should be addressed to author via email at benagoldstein@gmail.com.

Ben Goldstein and Mac Taylor

Ben Goldstein is a consultant in communications and speechwriting at the U.S. Department of State in Washington, D.C. He graduated from Pomona College in 2013 with a BA in English. He and Mac Taylor met on the first day of high school in Latin class, and the two quickly became best friends and eventual writing partners. Their projects include a screenplay set in 19th century Mexico and a half-hour comedy pilot. Goldstein has also worked as a freelance reporter, and has been published in *NPR*, *The New York Daily News*, and *Gothamist.*

Mac Taylor is a Los Angeles resident who works as a writers' assistant on the Fox sitcom *Grandfathered*. He graduated from Wesleyan University in 2013, where he majored in History. He and Ben Goldstein met in Latin class on the first day of 9th grade.

The Zone Ranger was originally produced as part of the Playwrights Festival at Harvard-Westlake School in North Hollywood, California on April 24, 2009. It was directed by James Elden (as James Sauer); the set was by Rees Pugh and Christopher Michael Moore; the costumes were by Lisa Peters; the lighting was by Ben Barad; the sound was by Jacob Swanson. The producer was Christopher Michael Moore. The piano player was Jake Staahl. The cast, in order of appearance, was as follows:

Kurt Curtis	Ben Platt
Charley	Arielle Basich
Simon	Daniel Rothberg
Woman #1	Brittany Richmond
Woman #2	Tess Hatch
Doctor	Alex Valdez
The Mayor	Chase Morgan
Bimbo/Perkins	Ariana Sopher
Marla	Kathryn Gallagher
Walter Crimelord	Daniel Lundberg
Favre	Jason Hirschhorn

The Zone Ranger premiered in *PL.A.Y Noir* and was produced Punk Monkey Productions at the Actors Workout Studio in the North Hollywood Arts District in June 2012. It was directed by James Elden. The lighting design was by Will Adashek. The cast, in order of appearance, was as follows:

Kurt Curtis	James Elden
Charley	Andrew J. Hillis
Simon	Jim Shipley
Woman #1	Anna Laura Singleton
Woman #2	Elisa Dyann
Doctor	Christopher Flowers
The Mayor	Michael C. Silva
Bimbo	Aubrie Wienholt
Marla	Sarah Kelly
Walter Crimelord	Adam Hunter Howard
Favre	Damon Pfaff
Perkins	Roxanne Jaeckel

CHARACTERS:

> **KURT CURTIS:** A private dick. The hero.
> **CHARLEY:** An old bartender, has known Kurt for years.
> **SIMON:** A busboy at the bar. Looks up to Kurt.
> **WOMAN #1**: Young, beautiful, educated. Interested in Kurt and his tale.
> **WOMAN #2:** Older, mother type figure.
> **DOCTOR:** Middle aged, intellectual man.
> **THE MAYOR:** A buffoonish middle aged man with a penchant for women and oysters.
> **BIMBO:** An attractive lady who's cozy with the Mayor.
> **MARLA:** The Mayor's darkly beautiful young secretary. A femme fatale.
> **WALTER CRIMELORD:** Young, charming, ambitious entrepreneur who always gets what he wants not matter what the cost.
> **FAVRE:** Kurt's longtime partner and best friend.
> **PERKINS:** A private detective and Kurt's friend.

Scene I

Kurt Curtis, early 30s, haggard looking, is sitting at a bar drinking. Slow jazz plays in the background, and the stage is swathed in a soft blue light. Two women and a doctor sit near him.

KURT: *(To audience.)* Hey there, maverick. It's good to see some folks around here with smiles on their faces. I haven't been sleeping recently...It's been two weeks since Favre was whacked.

WOMAN #1: Favre you say? Who's that?

KURT: Only the bravest man I ever knew in my 15 years on the job. *(To bartender.)* Give me one more, Charley.

WOMAN #2: Ooh, you're a cop?

KURT: Hey, do I look like any old Jake? Hell no. I'm a private dick. Favre was my partner.

WOMAN #1: Oh, I'm sorry. Does this dick have a name?

KURT: He's got two, honey. I'm Curtis...Kurt Curtis.

WOMAN #2: That name doesn't really roll off the tongue.

KURT: I know. That's why I had to work twice as hard to get where I am today. I got a bald spot on the top of my head from banging against the glass ceiling so hard.

DOCTOR: Well, Mr. Curtis, that gig must be a real gas.

KURT: Gas don't even begin to cover it.

WOMAN #1: Oh?

The bartender, a portly old man named Charley, looks at Simon, a young busboy. Their attention perks up.

CHARLEY: Eh, Curtis, what's got you lookin' so blue?

KURT: Well, Charley, misses, Doctor, Simon—

SIMON: Yes, Sir!!!

KURT: What I seen these past two weeks—no man should see. It makes me sick just thinkin' about it. Sick enough to make a man lose faith in everything good and sacred in this world. Cuz after you look evil in the face, you ain't the same man anymore. You can go home everyday and kiss your girl on the cheek, but it just ain't the same...cuz after you seen the horrors I seen, nothing looks right anymore.

WOMAN #2: I may be a dame, but I'm a tough one. Let's hear it, Curtis.

DOCTOR: I figure I must see worse things everyday in the operating room.

SIMON: Yeah, Mr. Curtis, it can't be that bad!!! Let's hear the scoop.

KURT: Okay, then. It's your funeral.

Lights over the bar go dark.

SCENE II

S.R. lights up on the Mayor's office. The Mayor, early 50s, is sitting behind his desk with a cigar in his mouth and a Bimbo on his lap. He is tickling her and feeding her oysters with a spoon. His assistant, Marla, waits patiently.

KURT: *(Voice-over.)* It all started down at city hall.

MARLA: Mr. Mayor?

MAYOR: What is it, Marla?

KURT: *(Voice-over.)* The dame's Marla...the Mayor's assistant.

MARLA: I have the proposal from the Ad-Hoc Council.

KURT: *(Voice-over.)* The goofy lookin' man's the Mayor...he's about to speak.

MAYOR: I see. What does it say?

MARLA: Well sir, it's a proposal to re-zone a current L.A. neighborhood boundary—over in Northern Westwood. It'll remove the historic district status from the residential areas.

MAYOR: Are you serious? How is that even possible?

MARLA: Well, under our current Euclidean zoning laws, certain areas are designated as residential, commercial, etc., and theses boundaries are fixed. The Ad-Hoc Council is proposing changing these laws to incentive based zoning, which allows developers to build any type of structure as long as it meets established urban development goals.

MAYOR: Christ, Marla...I knew this day would come, I just didn't think it would be this soon. Who's in charge of this ad-hoc council?

MARLA: A young entrepreneur...Walter Crimelord.

MAYOR: We're a dying breed, Marla...no one else in this town has scruples anymore. Well, bring him in already.

MARLA: Right away, sir.

Marla exits. She re-enters with an imposing man in his 20s, Walter Crimelord.

MARLA: Sir, this is the head of the Ad-Hoc Council, Walter Crimelord.

Marla and Walter exchange a furtive glance.

MAYOR: Welcome, Mr. Crimelord.

The Mayor gets up from his desk, and it is revealed that he is only wearing boxers.

MAYOR: Pardon my appearance, my friend was just pleasuring my behind the desk. You look like a supple young lad, and I have some extra oysters...care to join in?

WALTER: No, thanks, sir, I'm fine.

MARLA: Here's his resume, sir.

She hands the mayor a sheet of paper.

MAYOR: *(Reading off sheet.)* Walter Crimelord: Owner of "Walter's Brothel", Head of "Walter's Bookies", Head of "Walter's Racketeering Operation", Head of "Walter's Smugglers". Hmm, Mr. Crimelord, I was initially skeptical of your plans, but I like you. Don't ask me why, but I'm willing to hear you out on your council's proposal.

WALTER: Thank you, Mr. Mayor. I came to you to discuss the possibility of building an ice rink in your fair city.

MAYOR: What? Ice? Rink? Get the hell out of here!

WALTER: Sir, hear me out. From here to Coyote Hills, this place is a desert, a Godforsaken wasteland of fire and brimstone. What good are historic districts when history is trampled upon by vixens of the night and those lousy trouble boys? You see, Mr. Mayor, reverence is a thing of the past in this city. Yet from this ash we can create life...a fledgling, tenuous hope for something better. What is the perfect antidote to the fire that eats away at the City of Angels? Ice, my friend! Frozen water! Whatever you want to call it, that is why we're building an ice rink. And if you can't see that by now, then God help you.

MAYOR: I see. What you say is true. Perhaps the ends justify the means.

WALTER: Thank you, Mr. Mayor, I knew you'd understand. Ready to sign?

MAYOR: My boy, this is an unprecedented piece of legislation, and I could take a lot of heat from both the progressives and the unionists for this...we need time to talk this over. How about you come to my villa at Big Bear this weekend? We can go spearfishing and condor shooting at the hunting grounds.

WALTER: Thanks, but no thanks, sir.

MAYOR: I see. Well, where do I sign?

KURT: *(Voice-over.)* Now, I wasn't clued in on any of this...and when I found out, it appeared to be too late.

SCENE III

Kurt comes into his apartment with a weary look on his face. He hangs up his coat and tie and sits down on his couch. All of a sudden, a loud knock is heard at the door.

FAVRE: *(Outside the door.)* Lemme in! Curtis! I'm dyin'!!!

Kurt bolts to the door and opens it, catching the almost limp body of Favre in his arms.

KURT: What the hell happened?! You're bleeding everywhere!!!

FAVRE: I know, Kurt. I'm hurt...I'm hurt real bad.

KURT: No!!! Favre!!!

FAVRE: I'm sorry, Kurt...it's real bad this time...I gotta tell you something, I found something out...that's what they done me in for.

KURT: Tell me! What?

FAVRE: The proposal at City Hall...to rezone the historic districts...there's something about it that's fishy...

KURT: Okay, what else?

FAVRE: That's it. You have to promise me to stop them!!

KURT: I promise. Whatever crooked suit did this to you is gonna pay.

FAVRE: Thanks.

A long pause. Favre looks up at Kurt calmly but says nothing.

KURT: I...I thought you said you were dying.

FAVRE: I *am* dying.

KURT: Okay...but you're speaking more coherently than you were a few minutes ago. And you're not breathing as heavily either.

FAVRE: So? I'm still mortally wounded.

KURT: How do you know that for sure?

FAVRE: That's what the doctor said.

KURT: You've seen a doctor already? And why would he release you from the hospital if he said you were mortally wounded?

FAVRE: I told him that I needed to tell my buddy something—something important. About rezoning the historic districts. He realized the gravity of the situation, unlike you.

KURT: Okay...I'm sorry. Can I get you anything? Do you want ice or something?

FAVRE: No, I can bear it. I'm in the Lord's hands now.

SCENE IV

Lights up S.L. revealing the bar.

KURT: In retrospect, I'm pretty sure Favre wasn't mortally wounded. I came home from the office the next day, and he was still lying on the carpet, fully conscious.

DOCTOR: That is curious, to say the least. When did he actually die?

KURT: About two days later.

DOCTOR: Well, that's a pity. He could have received medical attention during that time.

KURT: He refused any help I gave him, insisting he that he was going to die any minute.

DOCTOR: Yeah, but you can always call the paramedics...

KURT: You and your castles in the air, Doc...anyways, as I was saying, I made a promise to Favre in his final days, and I intended to follow through with it.

WOMAN #1: How noble!

KURT: Listen, sister, I'm no saint. But when your partner gets bopped, the least you can do is find the man who did the boppin'.

CHARLEY: This is gettin' pretty grim...how 'bout one more round of gin?

KURT: Yeah, I could use some more of that eel juice, Charley...Now, where was I?

> ### *SCENE V*
>
> *Mayor's office. Kurt enters and sees Marla at the reception desk.*

KURT: *(To audience.)* Check out the gams on that broad.

MARLA: Hello.

KURT: Howdy, there. I'm looking to get an audience with the Mayor...would that be feasible?

MARLA: And just who might you be?

KURT: Curtis...Kurt Curtis.

MARLA: That name doesn't really roll off the tongue...

Kurt shushes her by placing his finger to her lips.

KURT: I'm an old friend...Tell him it's urgent.

THE ZONE RANGER   73

MARLA: Sorry, Curtis, but the Mayor doesn't have any friends.

KURT: That's not what I heard. In fact, I got some photographs with me that might suggest otherwise.

MARLA: Now, what's that supposed to mean?

KURT: Listen here, doll...

MARLA: It's Marla.

KURT: Hmm, Marla...sounds awfully like Christopher Marlow, the English dramatist and Shakespeare's contemporary.

MARLA: Yeah, my folks were huge fans of his.

KURT: Makes sense. Well, Marla, as I hope you're aware, I've insinuated that I have some incriminating photographs of Mr. Mayor, and I'm prepared to blackmail him.

MARLA: I think you're bluffing – let me see 'em.

KURT: You think I'd show my cards so early?

MARLA: Good point, Curtis. The Mayor's right this way.

KURT: Thanks, kid. You're too sweet. And by the way - I was bluffing.

Kurt walks past her desk and enters the Mayor's office, where the Mayor is sitting and eating oysters.

KURT: *(Voice-over.)* Now it was time for a bit of the Curtis magic. They don't teach you this in gumshoe school.

MAYOR: Yes, what is it?

KURT: Mr. Mayor, it's a pleasure to speak with you.

MAYOR: *(Looking up.)* Hey, I don't know you. You're a little old to be one of those silly new pageboys they've got here. *(He shouts offstage.)* Marla, who is this funny man?

KURT: Sir, I've traveled from the east on dispatch from the ailing President Roosevelt. Surely you've heard of the tri-annual city hall inspection? I'm assigned to each municipal edifice on the golden coast. You know, official business.

MAYOR: Well, my oriental friend, I don't know what that means, but I was in the middle of my oysters. Now, if you'll excuse me-

KURT: Mr. Mayor, we've gotten intelligence about your zoning plans, and frankly, it's causing quite a stir on the hill.

MAYOR: Ah, I'm not the man you're looking for. I don't understand a word of those laws. Just this week, the Ad-Hoc Council wrote another one: something about removing a historic district, or changing zoning boundaries, or opening up some real estate to build an ice rink...I dunno, it's all Greek to me!

KURT: Hmmm...yeah. You make it sound pretty complex. What's this about an ice rink?

MAYOR: A skating rink. You know, for the youth, the families.

KURT: I see, Mr. Mayor. In fact, I understand completely. Please go on.

MAYOR: The law's going to put an ice rink smack-dab in the middle of a whole bunch of homes. Not to worry though, these homes have families and youths, I already checked with the guy who's heading it up – Crimelord, I think he's named. So these families and youths will skate over at the rink, and it'll rejuvenate this city. Families, skating, some hustle and bustle, commerce! These are things a city wants, things a city needs. There's gonna be ice, you know – the perfect antidote to fire!

KURT: Thanks for the tip, sir. FDR appreciates your help.

MAYOR: Tip?

Kurt walks over to Marla's desk.

KURT: Listen, doll. How about I take you out for a smell o' the barrel?

MARLA: Well, maybe just one soda pop. I'm a lightweight.

He takes her by the arm and they exit.

SCENE VI

Kurt and Marla at the bar, now in red light. Charley and Simon are present.

CHARLEY: What you got there, Curtis? We don't serve any dish as pretty as this one.

SIMON: Here, here!

KURT: Hey, why don't you stick to makin' drinks, and I'll make the sweet talk, all right, Charley? *(To Marla.)* Now, tell me honey, what do you know about Incentive-Based Zoning?

MARLA: *(Surprised.)* What? Nothing...I'm just the Mayor's secretary.

KURT: You don't know anything about this Crimelord fellow?

MARLA: Not much. Only that he's trying to build an ice rink to attract families and youths to North Westwood.

KURT: Yeah. That's the line they're givin' out...but you did handle the mayor's paperwork concerning rezoning the area for incentive based development rather than Euclidean?

MARLA: I might've...what's it to you? How about I ask *you* a question, Mr. Professor?

KURT: Sure, I've got nothing to hide.

MARLA: What do you do for a livin'?

KURT: Oh, I wouldn't want to bore you with that.

MARLA: Is the life of Kurt Curtis really that boring?

KURT: Yep...if you're lookin' for excitement, you've shacked up with the wrong guy.

CHARLEY: Hey, lady, he's just pullin' your gams. You lose somethin', this guy will find it for ya.

MARLA: How about a broken heart?

CHARLEY: You must be new in town. Everyone knows Curtis here doesn't find the broken hearts, he does the breaking.

KURT: Give it a rest, Charley, you old boozehound. I make an honest living just like any other fella who comes into this stinkin' gin joint. Anyway, Marla, you look like you could break some hearts yourself.

MARLA: Why don't you try me?

KURT: Watch it, doll. Why don't you finish your drink?

Lights over the bar go dark except spot light on Kurt and Marla.

MARLA: Well, Mr. Curtis, if you're gonna order me around, I think I'll find something else for my night's entertainment.

KURT: Oh, yeah? What's a broad like you do for kicks? Besides breakin' hearts apparently.

MARLA: Oh, this and that. Not much for a girl to do in this town. Nothing but those dirty old gambling joints and flophouses...is that what you're into, Curtis?

KURT: Nope.

MARLA: This dick's sounding a little private. Here's an interrogation for the gumshoe: it's 10 o'clock. Friday night. What's Kurt Curtis up to?

KURT: I try to catch a picture at least once a week. Over at the Egyptian.

MARLA: Hmm, always with a pretty young lady, I assume, right?

KURT: Nope.

MARLA: Ohh, you're all alone in the dark?

KURT: I suppose. But there's usually quite a crowd.

MARLA: You don't mind sitting next to all those strangers?

KURT: I like it, I suppose....sitting in the dark. Not knowing who's around you, who they are...

MARLA: *(Leaning closer.)* What else do you like to do for fun in the dark?

KURT: Do you think I'm gonna spill it all right now?

MARLA: I don't cry over spilt milk.

KURT: Well, you're one of a kind, doll. Why don't you say we blow this joint?

SCENE VII

Same bar. Present day. Blue lights come up.

CHARLEY: That was the broad? Jeez, I must be gettin' old. I can't believe that was two whole weeks ago...feels like just yesterday.

SIMON: Mmm mm. Mr. Curtis does bring an awful lot o' those lady folk 'round here...'cept I just can't get this one out of my head for some reason.

KURT: Yep. This one was different...

CHARLEY: Wait, Mr. Private Dick Kurt Curtis wasn't actually dizzy with a dame now, was he?

WOMAN #1: She sounds like a regular old floozy if you ask me.

KURT: Listen, ladies, and you, Charley, you smoked sap. Kurt Curtis don't always got the bulge, but no bimbo ever bopped this bird. If you broads are gonna keep blowin' smoke and bumpin' your gums, then either you breeze on out or I'll take a bunk.

DOCTOR: Settle down now, Mr. Curtis. Why don't you tell us what happened next.

KURT: Alright, Doc. If you want the prognosis, I'll lay it on ya straight.

SCENE VIII

Kurt's apartment. Marla acts tipsy. Favre is on the floor, conscious but not saying anything. Kurt's gun is on the nightstand next to the couch.

KURT: *(Voice-over.)* The doll had tried to get me in to her canary nest on south Franklin, but I wasn't having none of it. It was 11 o'clock, and I wanted to be on my home turf.

MARLA: That was a blast, wasn't it?

KURT: Yeah, honey, a real hoot.

MARLA: That's a pretty scary looking gat you've got there.

KURT: That old thing? It's nothin', doll.

Kurt kisses her on the mouth. Passionately. Marla reaches for and grabs the gun on Kurt's nightstand, as she backs away.

MARLA: Now it's scary, isn't it, Private Dick Kurt Curtis?

KURT: What are you playing at, kid?

MARLA: I'm sorry, Kurt. I didn't think you'd be such a fool as to fall for a gal like me.

KURT: Well, it's your lucky day. Cuz you were right.

Kurt reaches for a gun of his own. Marla fires the gun, but nothing happens.

MARLA: What?

KURT: That's right. Blanks. Any self-respecting private dick always carries two guns. You think I'd leave one loaded lyin' around for a broad like you to snatch away? *(Kurt sits Marla down and keeps his gun pointed at her as he makes a call.)* Hey...it's Kurt. Yeah, you got him with you? Yeah, bring him on over. *(Hangs up the phone.)* You're in for a treat, kid.

MARLA: Kurt, I'm sorry. You don't understand.

KURT: Oh, I think I understand perfectly. Your heart is as cold as that ice rink you're trying to build.

Doorbell rings. Kurt opens the door, revealing Perkins standing behind a handcuffed Walter Crimelord. They enter.

THE ZONE RANGER 79

MARLA: Walter!

KURT: Marla, let me give it to you straight. I had my buddy Perkins- a private dick over at the Watercress Hotel, follow your friend Crimelord home today. Thank God for Perkins and his jungle cat stealth. Crimelord got what was comin' to him-- a sock in the jaw and a couple of these bracelets for good measure. Turns out you two aren't as clever as you thought. *(Looks at Walter.)* I know what you're up to over at City Hall. You and the goons on your ad-hoc council may have fooled the Mayor, but you ain't foolin' me. That zoning legislation's about the worst thing I've ever seen. To think that I man is capable of such evil -- that residential neighborhood is a historic piece of land, and I cringe at the thought of an ice rink chilling the warmth and beauty of those craftsman style homes. Well, sir, I'll have none of it. It's bad enough you're in cahoots with your brother-in-law who owns the real estate firm that would rake in the profits from that ice rink. But what really eats away at me is your total disregard for the stately architecture of the City of Angels.

WALTER: Is that really why you've got me tied up?

KURT: Hey, pal, I thought I told you to shut up. And Marla, you selfish broad, to swindle the Mayor for this lousy lowlife – I can't believe you.

MARLA: Kurt, you sap. Don't you get it – the world doesn't give a damn about swindling and selfish broads. I gotta look out for myself. And Walter and his brother-in-law. And now I have a question for you – at what point did you piece all of this together?

KURT: I work fasts, honey.

Doorbell rings again.

KURT: Oh, I bet that's your friend, the Mayor.

Kurt opens the door. The Mayor walks in, surveys the scene and looks confused.

MAYOR: Hey, Kurt – I thought you said this would be an oyster party.

KURT: Sorry, Mr. Mayor, that ended hours ago. But now that I have you here, you might want to smell what's been goin' on under your very nose.

MAYOR: I'm afraid I don't understand. Oh, and who's that man lyin' on the ground? He looks gravely ill.

KURT: That's my partner, Favre, a victim of these zoning laws and all the evil that they've caused.

MAYOR: Favre? Isn't that a football play—

KURT: Sir, this is 1944!

MAYOR: Ah, my mistake. My apologies.

FAVRE: It's okay, Mr. Mayor. I get it a lot.

Favre dies.

SCENE IX

Back at the bar. Silence ensues.

DOCTOR: That might be the most peculiar tale I've ever heard.

WOMAN #1: You showed so much bravery though, Mr. Curtis. You should be proud!

KURT: Cut it out, doll. At the end of the day all I got to show for this is a croaked partner and some silly old broad in the slammer.

WOMAN #1: Really? Are all women just "silly broads" to you, Curtis?

KURT: Listen. You can sit in this warm little gin joint listening to some crazy private dick mouth off and tell yourself it ain't nuthin...but I was there, honey! I stared into the blackness of the human soul and came back with my sight intact...Goddamn it! I swear, I wish I was blind, so I would never have to see another one o' you stinkin' broads again. It's torture I tell ya!

CHARLEY: Kurt, you're drunk. Stop before you say something you're gonna regret!

SIMON: Mr. Curtis?

KURT: What, kid?

SIMON: Well, you did save those Craftsman style homes, didn't ya?

KURT: Yeah, what's it to you, kid?

SIMON: Well, me and my momma live in one of those homes...just us and my nine brothers...we were gonna have to move out. Momma didn't know where, she said we might have to sell five of my brothers.

A pause. Everyone looks at Kurt.

WOMAN #2: Sounds like our young friend here may have more sense than any of us.

KURT: Thanks, kid. I'm...I'm glad I could be of help to you.

WOMAN #1: Mr. Curtis, I think you could be of help to me, too.

KURT: Really? You ain't mad with me after all I said?

WOMAN #1: I'd like you to buy me a drink.

KURT: Well, I'll see what I can do...ya silly old broad.

They all laugh heartily.

KURT: One malted liquor, Charley. Put it on my tab.

CHARLEY: You know, Curtis, I was just thinkin'...even though you stood up for what ya believed in with the zoning and whatnot, a new ice rink in town would be kinda nice.

SIMON: But, Charley, what about my five brothers?

CHARLEY: They could work the Zamboni!!

They all laugh.

THE END

The purchase of this book includes a private link to the film version of *Speak No Evil* by Michael W. Moon. Directed by James Elden.
https://vimeo.com/103158756 Password: KittenMalone
(Note: The password is case sensitive. We hope you enjoy the film).

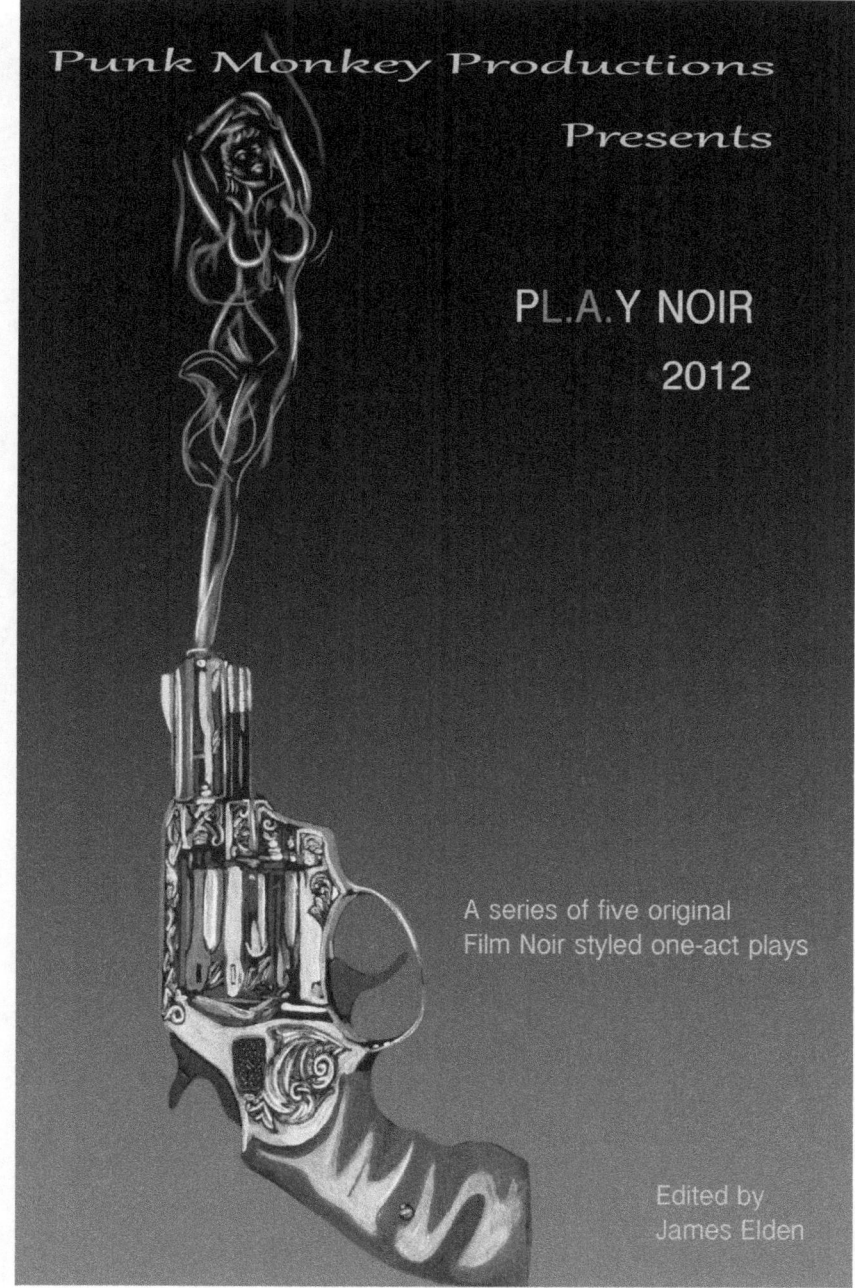

Also available from Punk Monkey Productions – PL.A.Y Noir 2012
Available on Amazon.

PL.A.Y Noir is an annual festival of one-acts that began in the spring of 2012. Punk Monkey Productions continues to announce a call for submissions each summer for the following year's production. We encourage playwright's to submit their Noir themed one-act as the festival grows. Playwrights and Noir fans alike, be sure to follow us and check in frequently for announcements pertaining to *PL.A.Y Noir* and Punk Monkey Productions on the sites below:

www.playnoir.com
www.punkmonkeyproductions.com

fb.com/playnoir
fb.com/punkmonkeyproductions

@playnoirla
@PunkMonkeyProds

@playnoir_la
@punkmonkeyprods

www.ingramcontent.com/pod-product-compliance
Lightning Source LLC
Chambersburg PA
CBHW031454040426
42444CB00007B/1101